Still Shakin' With Laughter

by Anthony Edey

with illustrations by Iris Edey

Still Shakin' With Laughter

By Anthony Edey
Illustrations by Iris Edey

First Printing October 2001. First Revised Edition February 2002
Second Revised Edition May 2012

ISBN-10: 0984983783 ISBN-13: 978-0-9849837-8-0

Printed in the United States

Additional copies of this book and of 'Life Lines' can be ordered from the publishers at:

IRIS' GARDEN
311 N Blake Ave.
SEQUIM, WA 98382
edeysqm@olypen.com

Book production: Magdalena Bassett, BassettStudio.com

Cover Art

The woodland violets on the cover were taken from a watercolour by Iris Edey. Iris' talent for botanical-style drawing and command of transparent watercolour have earned a large following, both for her originals and a selection of greeting cards.

Violets are traditionally associated with watchfulness and faithfulness, virtues of great importance in those who are called to serve as caregivers to Parkinson's Disease patients.

Dedication

For our children, Sandra Mary and Roger Brian,
so dearly loved and greatly admired for all their achievements.
Above all they have their Dad's sence of humour.

The last words he spoke the day he quietly slipped away
at home in September 2009, was a joke!
Yes, spoken nonchalantly with a typical
dry British sense of humour.

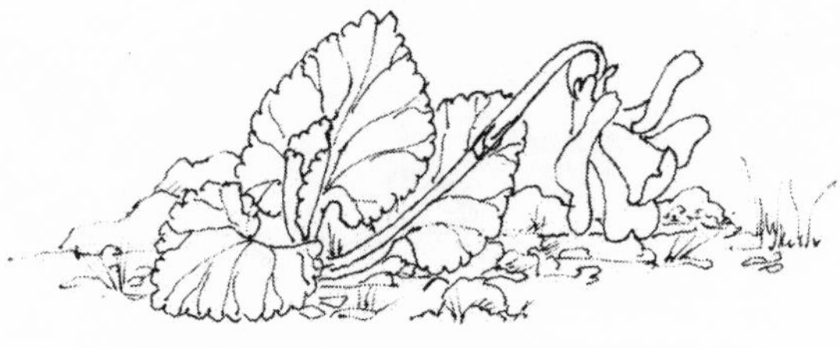

Contents

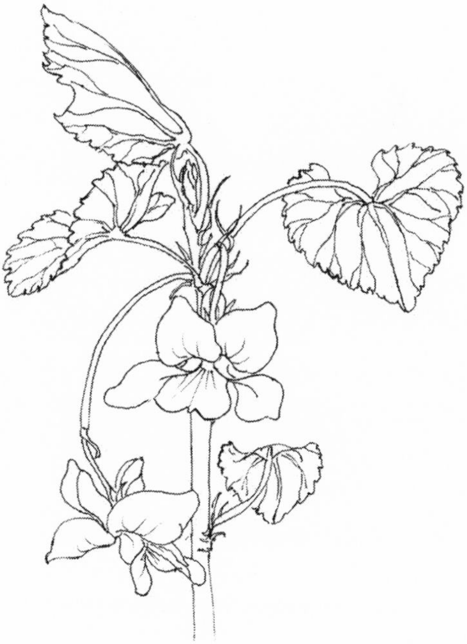

Introduction

As a consequence of being diagnosed with PD and, soon after, cancer, I found myself with a growing pile of paper covered in scraps of poems written to record my experiences and emotions and to help me deal with them. This process is captured in the poem on the opposite page.

In the year 2000, these 'scraps' became the book 'Life Lines' but the experiences did not stop then and another pile has been quietly taking shape. This booklet represents a first installment of that new collection and is focused exclusively on PD. It reflects the normal progression of the disease as well as, I hope, the facts that life goes on and that for every storm cloud on our horizon, there is certainly, somewhere, a giant silver lining.

—Tony Edey

Background

When high on Olympus the gods made their pick
Of who would stay healthy and who would get sick,
They fixed on my name by some dreadful mistake
To go on the list for the Parkinson's Shake.

These gods are quite careless, it seems pretty plain,
For just a year later they did it again.
A whopping big cancer the peril they chose
And planted it deep in the skin of my nose.

There followed a frenzy of treatment and care
For which I am grateful, but still I'm aware
My principle shields against shaking and tumor
Are family, friends and a keen sense of humor.

Through all of the stages of treatment and after
We've rarely been short of a reason for laughter.
So when I am tempted to rage or to curse
I fill in the time by composing this verse.

The following nine poems are snapshots of the PD life, with its many and varied abnormalities. For me, as they show, the worst impacts are usually brought about by some form of stress and are most marked in social settings.

PD's Plea

Just because I sometimes stumble,
Slur some words or seem to mumble,
Just because I have PD
Doesn't mean I'm not still me!

I don't mind that I walk funny
Take an age to count out money.
That's the thing most people see,
Not the person – just PD.

Locked inside this clumsy shell
Is the man you once knew well.
Though my nervous system's wrecked
I still have my self-respect.

Strange, heed this simple rhyme,
Give PD a bit more time.

It can be very helpful, as well as sometimes rather depressing, to see ourselves as others see us. The next poem describes the way a PD patient may very well look to another supermarket shopper – one who happens to be in a hurry.

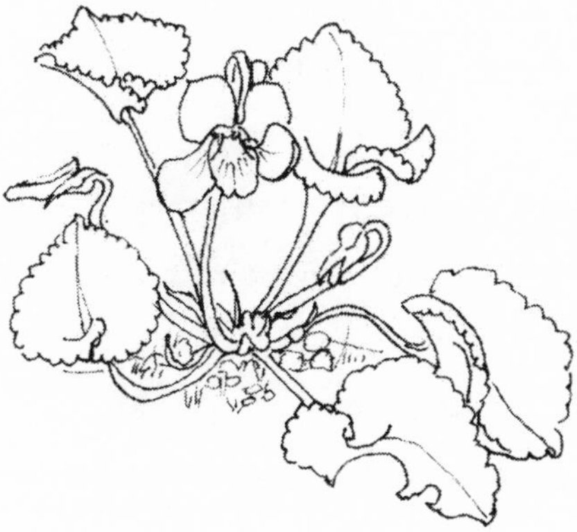

Checking Out

It's just forty minutes before they are due
And I have no doubt they'll be punctual, too.
I think if I hustle there's time (not a lot)
To dash to the store for the things we forgot.

It's all gone quite well, found it all the first time
So off to the checkout – must find a short line.
I see one that's open with only one man,
Not much in his basket, some fruit and one can.

He's taking for ever; I really must dash.
This silly old fool, though, keeps fumbling his cash.
He took half a lifetime just sorting each bill.
I'd be home by now if I'd not picked this till.

I've rattled my change, muttered curses, sighed deep,
Which just made him slower – I really could weep.
I think he's stretching it out just for me.
He knows I'm impatient – that's not hard to see!

At last he is done but he'd heard my loud sighs.
And slowly turned round, looked me straight in the eyes.
He wasn't as old as I'd come to expect
And though he had problems, his gaze was direct.

"Dear stranger, I'm sorry it took me this long.
It's so hard to wait when you're still young and strong.
But when you see someone with symptoms like these,
He probably has Dr. Parky's disease.

For him it's a battle to go to the store
And dealing with money is always a bore.
It means such a lot to a once vital man
To do his own shopping as long as he can.

Your wife will forgive you for taking so long
And you can explain to your guests what a wrong
Opinion you had of the dodderer who
Arrived at the check-out stand just before you".

Perceptions

When walking around you just stumble.
When counting out cash you just fumble.
While those who look on
Think your wits are half gone
And mutter and shuffle and grumble.

To them you are just a delay;
Some ancient who's got in their way.
But we know you're stuck
And it's just their bad luck –
They'll just have to wait while you pay.

They've not really met you or me.
What they've seen is mostly PD.
But we know it takes
More than tremors and shakes
To conquer life's jesters like We.

Shaky Old Parkinson

Thousands of pianists murder the classics,
Loath to admit that their talents are small.
But when you are older and things get no better
You suddenly realize the cause of it all.

Your friend Dr. Parkinson,
Shaky old Parkinson,
Somehow has stolen your talent away.
That terrible playing
(No talent displaying)
Can all be explained, through the eyes of today.

It all comes back clearly with razor-sharp hindsight,
Our playing was brilliant back then long ago.
It's only just lately we've started to lose it,
And, as we have mentioned, that's something we owe

To our Dr. Parkinson,
Shaky old Parkinson,
He who delights in frustrating our will.
But for his help we'd still ripple through Chopin,
And whistle through Liszt as though running down hill.

It's only just lately we're getting older
We've reached understanding of what has occurred.
The more we get shaky, the clearer our memories
Of musical triumphs and listeners stirred.

So our Dr. Parkinson,
Clever old Parkinson,
Brought us the gift of selective recall.
Rather than dwell on our shakier renditions
We dwell on the good bits or don't dwell at all!!

The Parkinson's Shake
(After Wordsworth)

I staggered, wobbly as a drunk
Who weaves his way from side to side
When suddenly my pills kicked in,
Just as the doc had prophesied.
My tremor stilled, the freezing eased,
I hardly felt the least diseased.

Precarious as a cliff-top walk,
These pills are life itself to me.
A PD cannot but rejoice at such a potent remedy.

For once when I was fast asleep
(In bed, I think but maybe not),
It came through loud and clear to me
What splendid treatment I have got.

Progressive as PD may be,
These pills are quite aggressive too,
And stop my tremor quite enough
That it's not obvious to you.

And so I'm left without a pain –
And then the shakes begin again!

A well-developed sense of the absurd is good preparation for Parkinson's Disease, as the next poems indicate.

Fasteners

There's nothing that's fast about old-fashioned fasteners.
Buttons and laces sure eat up my days.
It would be better to title them 'sloweners'!
They cause us frustration in so many ways.

Shirts with long sleeves and with smart-looking collars
Seem to have buttons all over the place,
Making our dressing a frustrating marathon,
Slowing us down to a toddler's pace.

These days a lot of the garments we wrestle with
Have as their fastenings a zipper or two.
Major improvements from buttons and buttonholes
Still not quite perfect whatever you do.

Zippers work perfectly, smoothly and swiftly
Except for the time when you have to zip quick.
Then some material jams in the zipper track
Foiling your efforts to make it unstick.

Then there are shoes for our lower extremities,
Way out of sight where our legs meet the floor.
Somehow we have to tie knots in the laces,
Ones that will last us for hours or more.

Here once again there's a modern convenience
Come to assist us in playing life's game.
Tie and untie with just one sweeping motion –
How did we manage before Velcro® came?

What can we do to avoid these embarrassments?
How to prevent these persistent defeats?
Maybe there's something to learn from the Arabs;
They seem contented just wrapped up in sheets.

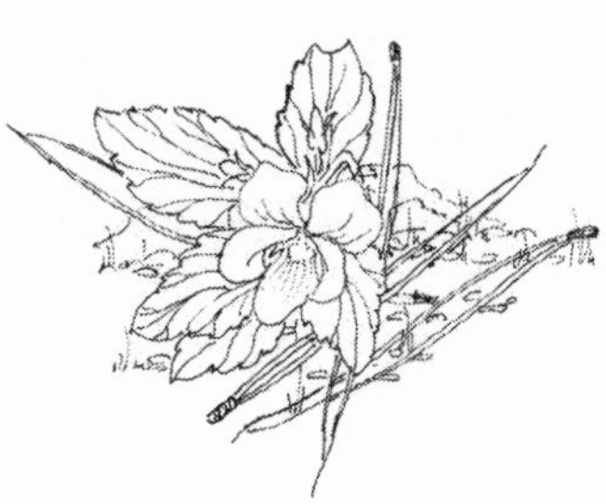

Choices

From day to day, or so it seems, mankind is learning fast
About the things that cause disease and those that help us last.
Indeed it seems if we can stay alive just long enough,
They'll even find a way to fix the common cold and cough.

From what we read in magazines or see upon the 'box',
Their fundamental work is slowly losing all the blocks
That bar our understanding of the workings of the brain
And why cells turn malignant and what's the cause of pain.

It's interesting to wonder just how this will all turn out;
If they will conquer Parkinson's – put cancer to the rout…
If all the usual killers can be conquered one by one,
How will we do our dying when our useful days are done?

We can't just live forever, think how crowded, what a squeeze,
So maybe in the end we'll have to choose our own disease.
I don't expect to see it but perhaps it will come true,
And just in case it happens, here is some advice for you

When making your selection, thing of choosing my matched pair.
Try Parkinson's for one, plus melanoma (if you dare).
They couldn't be more different in the way they do their work,
But this we know for certain, once they've got you they won't shirk.

Their complementary properties will keep you on the hop,
One may or may not bother but the other will not stop.
Old Parky's dead reliable, will never miss a day,
While fickle melanoma may just choose to stay away.

You never really know it's gone; it may just lie in wait
Until it sees its moment to return and terminate
Your slow but steady progress down the path of shake and quiver
By brief but surely fatal metastasis to your liver!

On second thoughts that doesn't sound the most attractive scene.
I think I'll reconsider what my choices might have been.
If Parkinson's and cancer have been conquered as we said,
There's really no good reason not to opt for life instead!

A Little Night Poem

Stumbling round the bedroom
In the middle of the night,
Trying to find the bathroom
Without any light.
It's the perfect moment
My muscles choose to freeze
And, (don't you know it?)
I think I'm going to sneeze.

Can't find my glasses
So everything's a blur.
Floorboard is creaking,
My wife's about to stir.
That's my biggest worry –
She needs all her sleep.
I just need the bathroom.
I really could weep!

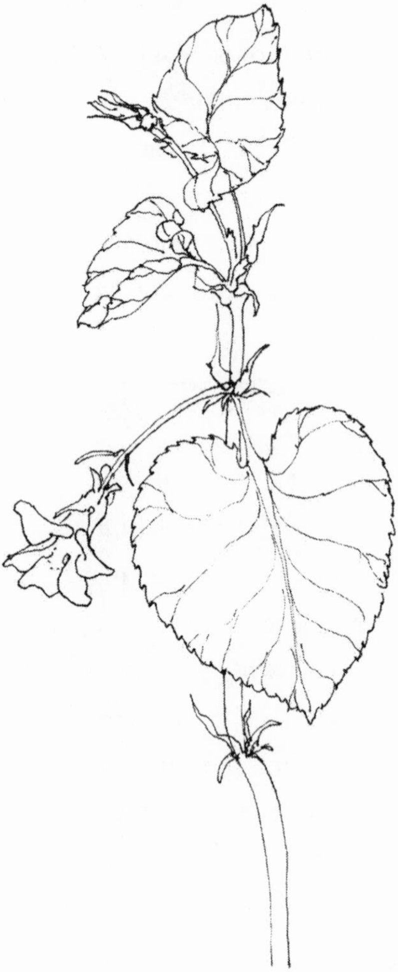

Senior Moments

Keeping names and faces straight
Helps you as you circulate.
Clarifies just who is who,
Who lives where and what they do.

All these useful things you know
Lubricate the social flow.
In their absence, sad to say,
Gaffes are never far away.

Carefully as I speak a name,
Then repeat it like a game,
By the time I've counted ten
All that data's gone again.

Seems that it's a flaw I face
In my basic database.
Now that I'm at last retired
Something vital's come unwired.

On that so-called database
There's a button marked 'ERASE'.
Long and wide and in the center,
Just where you would look for 'ENTER'.

So when I am introduced
To someone, the facts produced-
Name and face and other data,
Useful stuff to file for later.

All are filed, save that some glitch
Keeps that knowledge from its niche.
When you press the 'ENTER' knob
It's 'ERASE' that gets the job.

All that social knowledge won,
All relationships begun,
Fade to nothing in a haze
Not much use for future days.

So, dear friend, I'm pretty sure
We have talked at length before.
Without doubt I know your face,
But, if I could only place…

…Where you live and what you do,
If you have a wife, and who
Is she out of all this crowd,
(All so kind and all so loud).

So you see, just for a while
I can match you smile for smile.
'Til at last you're just a dream
And my smile becomes a scream.

If PD had a musical signature or theme it would probably be a rattle played by a pharmacist on a pill box. We function by courtesy of those expensive, multi-form and many-colored tablets and are often skeptical of their value and angered by their cost. In the end, though, they prove to be indispensable. The next group of poems looks at some of the ways of treating PD.

Sinemet®

When Requip® failed to do its work,
And there were hours of shake and jerk,
A little comfort could be got
From knowing I had one last shot.

About the best thought I could get
"At least I'm not on Sinemet.
These agonists can serve me still
As long as I have need of pills."

It dulled the pain and drew the sting
To know I'd not tried everything.
One drug remained untried as yet,
The great, Almighty Sinemet.

You hate to fire that final shot,
Simply, because it's all you've got.
If that one fails you're really stuck,
Unless, by some amazing luck…

They've dreamed up some new pill for you
To try when Sinemet is through.
Or maybe Medicare will deign
To Deeply Stimulate your brain.

But now PD's advance has brought
New urgency to that stale thought.
If Sinemet can do the trick
I'd better try it – pretty quick..

I can't waste time expecting news
Of brand new cures from which to choose.
I have a life to live today
And Sinemet will be the way.

How Ill Am I Anyway?

Everyone knows that PD is progressive
And well understand that there's not yet a cure.
But, thanks to those pills I can still – sort of – function
With PD a nuisance I have to endure.

The pills do their job very well (when I take them)
And stand like a wall between me and PD.
While we, though the battle is fought in our bodies,
Have no real idea just how ill we might be.

How much do we need to take all of these tablets?
Would life without Requip® be better or worse?
Perhaps without them I'd lose side-effects also
Plus finally close up the hole in my purse.

Well, take it from me it's not nice, 'cus I tried it.
I lasted four days without taking a pill.
Four busy days without Requip or Sinemet,
Four long, long days that remain with me still.

There was no nausea and not much light-headedness;
Those little treats I did not miss one bit.
Freezing and tremor were not that intolerable.
Maybe this 'treatment' would turn out a hit….

Except for the anguish in each of my muscles,
Trying to make do with no brain help at all.
Each in its own way appealing for something,
Shouting its woes like a 911 call.

It didn't take much of such strident sensations
To make it apparent I'd made the wrong call.
Suddenly all of those pill-popping problems
Became very clearly not problems at all.

Dosage

Who will greet the day tomorrow –
Jake the Shake or Steady Sam?
Nice if it were my decision,
Had some say in who I am.

One pill short and tremor's started,
Mostly noticed just by me.
But a more extreme omission
Has results that all can see.

First the tremor; hands and arms
May dance around like aspen leaves.
Then the aches and trouble walking,
Staggering as a drunkard weaves.

Take too many and your limbs
Are solid as Gibraltar's rock.
All your muscles start to feel
As frisky as a run-down clock.

All of this can be avoided
Just by keeping dosage right.
Then your pills can work their magic;
Morning times will feel just right.

Prescription

It seems to me that many pills
Treat mostly superficial ills.
Things people could endure but which
Instead make corporations rich.

I truly think that love heals more
Than all the potions from the store.
By love and care, a smile a touch
Love can accomplish just as much.

This then my new prescription! Take
A big 'Good Morning' when you wake.
One laugh per hour or maybe more-
There is no shortage in the store.

The experience of the years since diagnosis has convinced us that high on the list of factors which influence our health are those which might be called 'attitude' or 'lifestyle'.

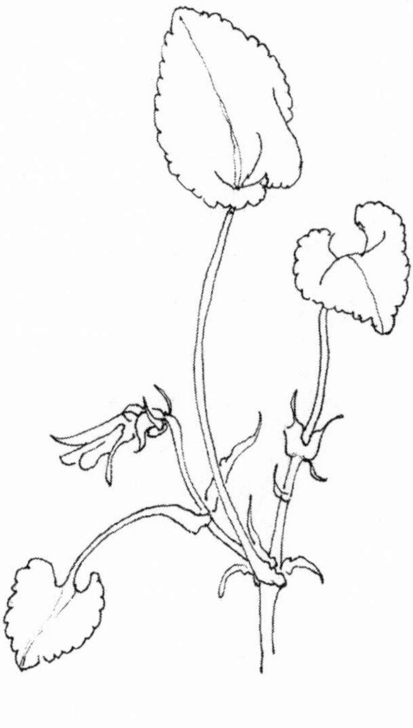

Let Go

I know a shrink who lives next door
And after 40 years he's sure
The way to deal these ills a blow
Lies in the act of 'letting go'.

So people who accept their state
And waste no time in cursing fate,
Find things to do and things to give
Will find their bodies yearn to live.

While those who take the other tack
And waste their time in looking back
Or curse their luck and pass out blame
Will have the symptoms just the same.

Eventually my end will come
And I just hope there'll be someone
Who'll feel that it is fair to say
"He lived life every single day."

The Faulty Engine

There once was an engine that lived in my head.
It started at birth and should run 'til I'm dead.
I find though that what's going on 'tween my ears
Sounds just as though someone's put sand in the gears.

I can't tell for sure why it's so out of kilter;
Perhaps there's some dirt in the nose or ear filter.
If cleaning them out doesn't make it run better
Maybe something's wrong with the whole carburetor.

You've given it pills and you've nursed it and cussed it
And now they've the means to go in and adjust it
So if it still falters whenever you park,
Your surgeon can fit you a new Deep Brain spark.

With all of this meddling you're lucky for sure
If what's in your head is no worse than before.
Your brain may be noisy and injure your pride
But try to ignore it – just enjoy the ride.

Your doctor's just doing the things that he can
But these things take time and he's only a man!
He needs to be cautious, no cause for alarm,
His very first promise was not to do harm.

Fads

In the paper every day
You will find a different way
Promised to improve your health
And inflate some guru's wealth.

Sure, we ancients need to watch
How we hit the wine or scotch.
And we hold the firm belief
We should limit lamb and beef.

Give up 'carbs' and, so we're told,
None will ever know we're old.
Shunning fats – or so some say –
Will extend your earthly stay.

Processed foods and tasty cheese?
Best go light on such as these.
But, and vital I would guess,
Is the need to worry less.

Keep from being too intense,
Never ration commonsense.
Eat the things that suit you best,
Simply eat them less and less.

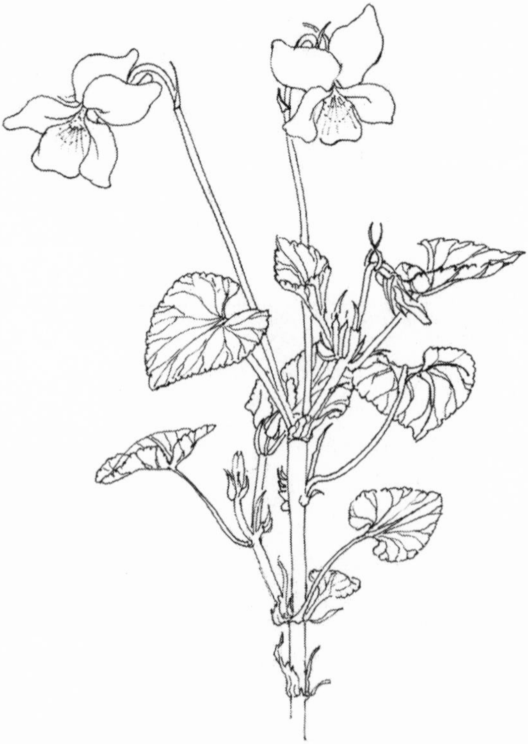

Time

Time is flying, time is finite
Time is clearly not enough.
Carefully though we try to hoard it
There's no way to store the stuff.

Well, at least we have the present,
Time on which we can rely.
Here alone we make a difference
All that future's just blue sky.

No collection of verse which claims to be even a little humorous would be complete without a few limericks.

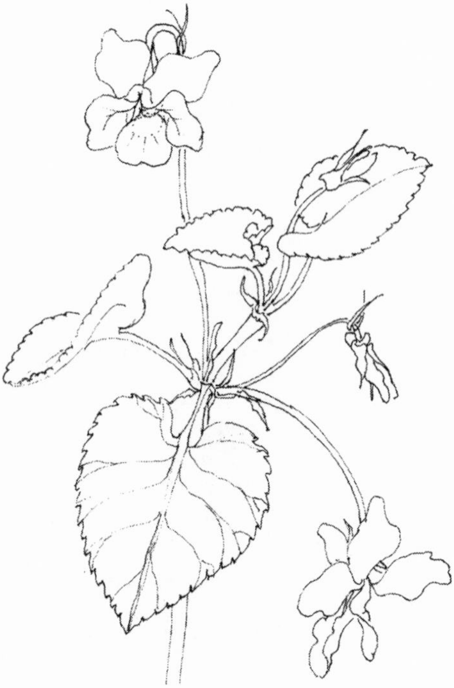

Short Thoughts

I

A Parkinson's patient with shakes
Said "I'll do whatever it takes.
But here's my dilemma:
The pills for my tremor
Cost more than the finest of steaks."

II

There was an old PD in Spain
Who left her green pills on the train.
She knew what to do;
Took one yellow, one blue,
And never felt nauseous again.

III

If all that pill-popping
Has PD a-stopping,
It's worth all the cost
And the appetite lost.
But what if they've taking
And you are still shakin'?

If the patients are the victims of PD, our patient care-givers are the heroes. I only hope that I have expressed that sentiment adequately somewhere in my verse: it is impossible in prose.

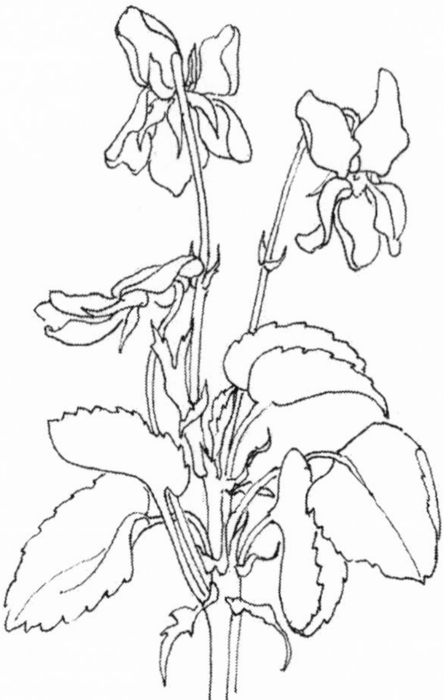

Touching Thoughts

There's a little parable
Buried in this dark disease.
Teaching us the things that harm;
Showing us the things that please.

Handling money hits me worst;
Brings on most unpleasant shakes.
People, though, have calming power;
Just a touch is all it takes.

So, you see, my addled brain
Still can grasp this basic truth –
Money has a stressful feel.
Touching people tends to heal.

Helping with Care

PD I have just begun a task,
Unimportant save to me.
Finishing it is all I ask,
Chalking up a score to me.

Yes, I know I'm pretty slow,
Take ten times the time I ought.
But, you see, that time is mine;
Mine to spend – or so I thought.

My great need is to complete
Each small task I start to do.
I'm not fearful of defeat;
I just want to see things though.

CARER I'm not an interferer
And I'm not the bossy kind.
But to stand and watch him struggle
Drives me half way out my mind.

That small job would take me seconds;
Save us both a lot of grief.
But PD is pretty stubborn
Has the very firm belief
That it should be his decision –
Soldier on or seek relief.

Vows

It's forty-two years since we stood in the aisle
In front of our families and friends,
We pledged to each other undying devotion
And prayed that our love would not end.

We pledged many things until death do us separate,
Promising gladly through poor times or wealth.
And then we committed to loving and cherishing
Through all conditions of sickness or health.

Poor times and sickness seemed all very distant
To us as we stood up together that day.
But all these years later they're suddenly relevant
Suddenly sickness has come here to stay.

Now those old promises take on real meaning.
Now are the basis on which we can stand.
I can still laugh, then, at what lies before us,
As long as I face it while holding her hand.

If these pages contain a message, it is to be found in this last poem. Life is shaky and risky and sometimes very difficult. It is, though, totally worthwhile and each of us still has something to give, however much we shake at the thought!

Intensive Care

We all know what ICU
Means to all the people who
Need its gadgets to survive:
Stay plugged in to stay alive.

I've a different ICU.
One I'll need to see me through
This strange life of shake and freeze.
Thank the Lord for such as these.

We're not joined by tubes or wires.
Patience is what she requires
Plus the wisdom to perceive
When to help and when to leave.

Maybe she'll not fend off death,
Start my heart or pump my breath.
Her IV's come through her smile:
Thus she makes it all worth while.

Silver Linings

What sort of person counts cancer a blessing
Or talks about Parkinson's doing him good?
Surely he'd have to be mentally challenged
Or bending the truth rather more than he should.

In fact it's quite true that these dreaded diseases
Have given me more than they've taken away
Beginning with one truly priceless awakening –
A constant delight in the joys of today.

And then there's retirement, much sooner than scheduled,
The door through which all of these joys can be found;
No motels or airports, delays or lost baggage,
No getting back home just in time to turn round.

Our days have been filled with a million enjoyments
From Outback Australia to walking our beach.
Some magical sailing, some PD support groups,
Each one is a bonus with lessons to teach.

Most valued of linings are surely the people,
Above all my wife on whose love I depend.
Add two caring children and grandchildren also,
Who couldn't care less if my nose has a bend.

So those evil clouds do indeed have bright linings
And shower us with blessings again and again.
There's plenty of wisdom in this simple saying:
'You never get rainbows without getting rain'.

Biography

Anthony and Iris Edey settled in the Pacific Northwest after 15 years in Central Africa followed by periods in Washington State, Colorado and Georgia. They were busily pursuing their respective careers in 1995 when a faulty arm-swing proved to be a sign of Parkinson's Disease. This news had only just sunk in when, a year later, a minor irritation on his nose proved to be a large and dangerous melanoma which required a total of six surgical procedures and some heavy radiation to subdue. It proved, however, impossible for Tony to continue his career as a globe-trotting mining consultant and he retired in 1997, many years earlier than planned.

These events were chronicled in a series of poems which record his reactions, hopes and fears and which eventually became the book 'Life Lines', created in collaboration with Iris who had established herself as a talented artist. Her distinctive style of exquisite botanical watercolor proved ideal for the book's cover and the text was enhanced by her drawings.

Although the melanoma had remained in remission, the Parkinson's Disease continued to progress. So too did the poetry, as evidenced by the 24 poems in this book.

Iris has published this new edition in memory of an extraordinary man; an army officer, underground mining engineer, beloved husband, father, and grandfather of Benjamin, Nathan, Hannah, Samuel, Megan, and Jamie. Also known as the Parkinson's Poet, he quietly passed away in September 2009.

Iris continues to paint watercolour flowers at her home in Sequim, Washington.

13202251R00039

Made in the USA
Charleston, SC
23 June 2012